The message of grace, if truly considered from scripture, is shocking! It is so shocking in fact that most believers still question just how far grace really goes. Surely, they say, there comes a point when God has simply had enough and will turn away and look for more worthy vessels. But what if God's response to our sin is to pursue, not turn away? What if His desire for us is much, much more powerful than our desire for the world and what if He intends to win our hearts with His overwhelming goodness and relentless pursuit?

It is with these thoughts in mind that my dear friend and co-laborer in Christ, Mathew Toller, has written this book. It is a small book full of big revelation and should be read, savored and wrestled with (and it will make you wrestle).

Writing from a rabbinical standpoint, Mathew challenges some very common thoughts on grace. But I assure you that he never drifts into "hyper grace"and that his treatment is thoroughly biblical. Mathew walks through scripture and unfolds, in very simple language, the radical nature of grace.

May you be encouraged by this book. May it awaken a desire to go after the God Who has always come after you!

David J. McDaniel
Youth With A Mission
Tokyo, Japan

Mathew Toller's book *Grace Undone* comes from the heart. It is his life story. But it is so much more. Mathew has a unique perspective as a rabbi and a missionary. I discovered new understanding of God's grace in these pages. The stories in this book brought the reality of God's unconditional love alive in a new and fresh way. I highly recommend this book on your reading list!

Tom Cole
Director, Pure Heart Ministries
Greenville, SC USA

I met Mathew while my wife and I were living in Budapest, Hungary. We quickly became friends and saw in this young man a passionate lover of Yeshua! We often had discussions over dinner, talking about such things as grace, forgiveness, acceptance, and how to reach the Jewish people that we had such a heart to see come to salvation. We were Mathew's YWAM school leaders, and were blessed to be a part of his journey in re-discovering the amazing revelations of "Messiah in me, the hope of glory." I found his book to be a powerful story of redemption and intimacy between a loving Father and a son eager to imitate Him. I highly recommend this book to anyone seeking to experience transforming love, and the incredible power of His grace as we walk in our new identity!

Stewart Lieberman
Messianic Pastor, Or Chaim Congregation
Golden, CO USA

C.

Mathew Toller is an Outstanding Communicator and Teacher whose revelational insights are impacting people groups around the globe. The authority and authenticity with which Mathew expounds foundational truths are both life-giving and transformative. At The Forge School of Faith in Llanelli, which welcomes the young from many continents and the not so young like myself, I have experienced and observed how compelling this teaching is in reshaping misconceptions about God and refueling a passion to embrace clear biblical principles as a way to unlock understanding of your own identity and purpose. This book will lead you to be surprised by "Grace" and the stunning significance of "Sacrifice" in a shaking world where everyone needs to know their true worth.

Reverend Vivien Firth
Speaker, Christian Mentor and Life Long Learner!
North Yorkshire, United Kingdom

Laughter, good food, and stories — that is how I know Mathew. Reading his book brought new insight and joy. Mathew is a fantastic story teller, and yet again made my heart breathe deeper and increase my desire to draw closer to Jesus.

Monika Avakian
Youth With A Mission
Germany and beyond

Mathew was a gift in my life during a season when I was crying out to the Lord to send me a man whose heart burns for the Lord. God's answer came in the form of a full-bearded Jewish-American Messianic Rabbi with a level of witty but sometimes sarcastic humor. Little did I know this man with a big heart and deep revelation from the Lord would have such a powerful impact in my life through the message of grace. A life of freedom that is to be experienced through God's grace is far more radical than we're comfortable with at times. I've had the privilege of walking closely with Mathew for the past six plus years and I have seen firsthand the level of impact that this message has had in his life and so many around him. It has been my prayer that this message be penned into a book to bless the masses. And I'm so thankful that it came out so beautifully. Be warned though, this book may wreck your life. As Mathew testifies in the book, living this message out is hard at times but be reassured, it is beyond amazing. May this book draw you deeper into the heart of God who desperately longs for his children to receive his unfathomable love and grace.

Sungwoo Park (ph.D)
Friend and Businessman
Seoul, Republic of Korea

Whether this is your first or tenth book on grace, Mathew's insights will have a profound impact on your understanding of the whole canon of scripture and the nature and character of God.

Joe Biggs
West Sussex, United Kingdom

Grace Undone

A Rabbi's Pursuit in Understanding
God's Ultimate Gift

By Rabbi Mathew Toller

Grace Undone: A Rabbi's Pursuit in Understanding God's Ultimate Gift
Published by the Klug Publishing Group, LLC
Copyright © 2018 by Mathew Toller

Printed in the United States of America.

Some names and identifying details have been changed
to protect the privacy of individuals.

First Edition

ISBN 978-0-9995870-0-3

All quoted scripture verses are taken from:

The NEW KING JAMES VERSION (NKJV) ®
Copyright© 1982 by Thomas Nelson, Inc.
Used by permission. All rights reserved.

Grace Undone: A Rabbi's Pursuit in Understanding God's Ultimate Gift
is a publication of the:

Klug Publishing Group, LLC
1136 Union Mall Ste 301
Honolulu, Hi 96813-2711

For bookings or general communications with the author,
you can email klugpublishinggroup@gmail.com

Cover Design by Hanna Yang

Author photo by Lily Wang
www.philipandlily.com
For photography bookings, email:
lilywangphoto@gmail.com

ACKNOWLEDGMENTS

With my deepest gratitude I am beyond thankful
for the group of friends who have supported me in every step.
Thank you to all the people who encouraged me, prayed for
me, and supported me to pursue the call of God upon my life.
Finally I must thank my father for his godly influence, and no
book would be complete without acknowledging
my Jewish mother, who made sure I knew her opinion
with each and every paragraph.

Contents

Prologue

In the 1980s, the chief rabbi of Jerusalem went to the Vatican to visit the pope for the first time. When the rabbi, entered the pope's office, he was in awe of the simplistic yet beautiful artwork from various masters that adorned the walls. The pope sat behind a big oak desk and the rabbi sat down in a plush chair. As the two engaged in lively conversation, the rabbi noticed a golden telephone sitting on the pope's desk.

"Your Holiness, what is that golden telephone for?" the rabbi asked.

The pope smiled and said, "That phone is how I talk to God. Whenever I have a problem or a question I simply pick it up and speak with Him." The rabbi was impressed, so he immediately asked if he could use the phone to talk with God. The pope said, "Sure, no problem, but it's a little expensive."

The rabbi was so excited. "Money is no object—I just want to talk to God!"

The rabbi picked up the phone and spoke with God for five minutes. As he hung up the phone, the rabbi had a huge smile on his face. "Thank you so much! That was the most amazing conversation of my life. How much money do I owe you?"

The pope, also smiling, said, "Well, you spoke to God for five minutes, so I'm sorry to say that it's going to cost you five thousand dollars."

The rabbi grinned. "No problem! My conversation with God was so great and I'll gladly pay."

After many months, the pope was traveling the world. He made a trip to Israel and decided to visit his friend, the chief rabbi of Jerusalem. As the pope entered the rabbi's office, he was amazed at the humble office that was filled with artifacts from the

Holy Land. When he sat down, he noticed a golden telephone sitting on the rabbi's desk.

"You have a golden phone!" the pope exclaimed.

The rabbi laughed and said, "Well, after I knew you had one, I had to get one."

The pope then asked, "I have been traveling the world for such a long time, so would it be possible to use your phone? I have so many things I need to talk to God about." The rabbi gladly allowed the pope to use the golden phone.

The pope talked on the golden phone for two hours. When he was finished, the pope thanked the rabbi. "Thank you so much for letting me talk with God. I so needed that conversation. I talked to Him for two hours. I'm afraid to ask, but how much do I owe you?"

The rabbi thought about it for a moment and then said, "Fifty cents."

The pope jumped to his feet, shouting, "Fifty cents? Fifty cents? How can it only cost fifty cents? You spoke for five minutes and it cost five thousand dollars. I spoke for two hours, so how can it only cost fifty cents?"

The rabbi shrugged his shoulders and said, "From Jerusalem, it's a local call."

In all of our lives, there are things we learn, know, and understand that have influenced our own worldview about God. Because we all come from different cultures and have varying views, we arrive at common truths very differently. Our belief, faith, and the exercising of that faith also varies greatly. Sometimes we must return to the source, to rediscover simple truths that have been lost. I hope the following will bring new life to your heart, mind, and spirit.

Introduction

In the beginning, God created the heavens and the earth, and it was good. Everything that God made was very good, from the first day of creation to the last. In His grand finale of all creation, God created man. *God created us.* Even though God declared that we were very good and He formed us in His image, we still struggle to accept the simple truth about our true worth—to know whom we are in Him. Since the days of Adam and Eve, the battle over understanding our identity as children of the most high God has been raging in every single one of us. We want to discover our true value, as it is one of the largest driving forces in our lives.

Why is it such a struggle for us to acknowledge that we are children of God and our true value lies in His creation of us? Is it because we have fallen so far from our unique creation that we believe the worst about ourselves even though God has declared us the best? God's greatest desire for us is to know Him, to know His ways, and to know who we are in Him. When the world fell further away from His ways, God called one man, Abraham, to be the source of reintroducing His truth to humanity. It is through Abraham, Isaac, Jacob, and later, through the very hand of Moses, that God granted us His Living Word. Within the pages of the Torah (the first five books of the Bible), we find the very revelation of the tree of life that He has always wanted for us.

Often as I travel the world, I am asked about the Jewish perspective of the Bible. As a Messianic rabbi, it is a common request. Over the years, I have been preparing different messages on what I felt were the most important teachings, instructions, and revelations that God had given to Israel since that day when He first called my ancestor, my great-great-great... grandfather

Abraham. He was told to leave all he knew and go to a land that would be revealed to him later. However, of all my teachings, the most important teaching would have to be the message of grace.

Grace is the greatest of God's gifts, not just to Israel but also to the whole earth. The revolutionary truth of God's grace has the power to undo every work of the enemy in a single moment. Though grace may sound simple, the truth of this revelation has been misconstrued over time. Even as a Messianic rabbi, I am a Jewish believer in Yeshua ("Jesus" in Hebrew) who has been trained to be a pastor, I struggled to understand this most important foundation of our faith. After the truth of grace entered my heart, mind, and spirit, it took another ten years before I could truly teach on it. The revelation of God's grace came in an instant, but for me to gain an understanding of grace, it needed to become my life's passion.

Psalm 51:1-2

A Prayer of Repentance
To the Chief Musician. A Psalm of David when Nathan
the prophet went to him, after he had gone in to Bathsheba.

1 Have mercy upon me, O God,
According to Your loving kindness;
According to the multitude of Your tender mercies,
blot out my transgressions.
2 Wash me thoroughly from my iniquity,
And cleanse me from my sin.

PART 1
My Story

Revelation of Sin

I am one of three siblings; I have an older brother and a younger sister, so I have the honor of being a middle child with all of its rights and privileges. I was raised in a religious home where we went to an evangelical church on Sundays and Wednesday nights, a traditional conservative synagogue on Friday nights, and a Messianic congregation (a congregation of Jews and Gentiles who believe in Jesus but keep the Jewish and Biblical traditions) on Saturdays. Needless to say, I embraced the many facets of both the Christian and Jewish faith as a Messianic Jew.

Growing up, I was open to spiritual things. I have no memory of *not* knowing who Yeshua was. From the first time I ever heard His name, the reality of the Messiah rang as truth in my heart. However, when I was only seven years old in Orange County, California, I was already living a life of sin. Not only was I doing what was wrong on purpose, I was the perfect two-faced child. Whenever I was around adults, especially my friends' parents, I was nearly perfect. These parents were always telling their children to behave more like me. The other kids would look at me with daggers in their eyes. They knew what I was like when no adult was looking.

In primary school, I was fiercely independent. With a neighborhood friend, I would sneak into my second-grade classroom to steal odds and ends from the teacher's desk. My favorite thing to steal were scratch-and-sniff stickers. Our families lived in the same condominium complex, and we had a secret hideout near the railroad tracks where we had built a little fort. My friend and I would fill our fort with our illicit treasures, the greatest of which were pornographic magazines my friend stole from their father.

One afternoon, as I was out playing, I bumped into one

of my older brother's friends, Joey. I had never spent time with Joey before, but on that day, I invited him to check out our secret hideout. Once inside and out of sight of any adult, I pulled out the magazines. I was so proud to show them off to an older boy. He took one look at the cover, stared directly into my eyes, and said, "God doesn't want you to look at this!"

At that exact moment, as I held the magazine that was filled with pictures of naked women, I realized I had sinned against God. I had always heard about sin at Sunday school, but this was the first time that I understood I had sinned. At that moment, I knew what sin actually was. It was a revelation so deep that I felt as if my very soul was covered with filth. It wasn't just the act that was wrong or something I shouldn't have done because my parents wouldn't have approved. Instead, it was a deep chasm of longing that I had wronged God, my best friend in the world, and desperately needed to fix it, but I didn't know how.

I asked my brother's friend what I should do, and Joey said, "Let's throw them away immediately." Even though the magazines belonged to my friend and not to me, we tore them in half, crumpled them up, and chucked them over the nearest wall as if we were two young King Josiahs. As the magazines disappeared from sight, it was as if a huge weight had been lifted from my shoulders and I felt clean for the first time.

The Call

In the summer of 1984, I went to Camp Cedar Crest for the first time at the age of nine. Located in the scenic San Bernardino Mountains, the camp became my spiritual home and a place of great acceptance, learning, and encountering the Spirit of God. I attended that camp every summer and winter for eight years. There were worship services every morning and evening, devotions and quiet times, and camp competitions in the afternoon. I'm proud to say that I was the belly-flop champion more than once.

Out of all of my memories of Camp Cedar Crest, I will never forget the Thursday morning service of my very first camp. In a sanctuary filled with scores of nine- to twelve-year-old kids, the special camp speaker began to preach about God's calling for our lives. He asked if anyone felt as if God was calling them to go into full-time ministry and if so to please stand up. I shot out of my chair, unable to contain the feeling of God rising-up inside of me. A volcano erupted in my stomach as I stood there before what seemed like thousands of other campers. I thought for sure that every child would be on their feet, but only four kids stood up. At that moment, I knew I was destined to walk with God.

I was never the same after that encounter with God. I became more and more committed to God, to the church, and to living what I thought was a holy, religious lifestyle. I remember practicing worship in my bedroom so I would have the courage to raise my hands during the praise service in my youth group. I tried to stop being a two-faced child and even regularly volunteered to work with mentally disabled kids during my lunchtime at school. My sudden change in attitude and behavior separated me from the other boys, as I was no longer interested in doing the things I knew to be wrong.

While I was a middle and high school student, I continued to pursue my love for God. I read my Bible and tried to understand the mysteries it contained. One time, I wrote my own commentary on the Book of Revelation. Faithfully, I continued to go to church and youth group every Wednesday and Sunday. I also became the Shabbat School teacher (think of Sunday school but on Saturdays) for younger children at our Messianic Jewish congregation. I did all these things always believing in my heart that I was being prepared to go into full-time ministry for Yeshua.

Growing in God

By the time I had graduated high school, I was well on my way to living a life in ministry. I enrolled at CSU, Sacramento, in Political Science with an emphasis in International Relations, which allowed me to continue my growth in God. I was part of several of the university's Christian fellowships. I helped plant a local evangelical church in the center of town in Sacramento and was actively involved in planning evangelistic outreach initiatives. I served as president of our local Community Service Club and regularly volunteered at a center for children who had cancer. I believed I was pursuing God whole-heartedly. This isn't to say that I didn't have struggles with relationships, coming of age issues, or difficulties from my childhood still haunting me. I had personal sins I needed to overcome, but God made Himself so real to me that I could never deny His existence or His love for me.

I am so grateful for the lifelong friendships that God gave me during my university years. My roommate, Paul, taught me the value of worship, prayer, and listening to God's voice. I had friends, John and Kymm, who had gotten married young (they are still married and have two amazing children) but were filled with wisdom. They always accepted me for who I was and taught me the value of serving, the gift of giving, and hospitality. Through the invitation and guidance of an amazing pastor, Johnny Z, all of us became leaders in the new church in the heart of downtown

Sacramento. During that time, I had only thought of myself as a teacher, worshiper, and intercessor. I never saw myself as an evangelist until Pastor Johnny came to my dorm room in the spring of 1996 and turned my world upside down.

I will never forget that afternoon. I had finished my classes for the day and was nervously waiting for my pastor to arrive. I had never hosted my pastor in my simple dorm room before. I was surprised to see both my Pastor Johnny and his wife, Jeanie, but I invited them in and they sat down on the bed. They told me that they had been praying for someone to become the director of evangelism in the church. Essentially, that person had to ensure that every ministry had a form of outreach for sharing the gospel. I was certain that I must have been their fifth or sixth choice, so I asked, "How many others had turned down the role before you approached me?"

Pastor Johnny smiled. "You are our first choice, Mathew."

I was blown away. He and his wife had been praying when God specifically put me in their hearts to take on this position.

After praying and fasting for a couple of days, I realized that God wanted me to step out of my comfort zone and become the church's director of evangelism. God showed me that I had been limiting myself and my personal calling. At first, I was humbled with this newfound revelation, but after a few months I began to internalize my new position as proof of God's love and acceptance of me. Not wanting to disappoint God, I tried everything in my power to become more holy. I never missed a church service or a prayer meeting. I allowed my studies to be second to any church function and position as the director of evangelism. In my zeal, I was separating myself from anything I thought was worldly, such as secular music, university parties, and non-Christian friends. I only wanted to be accepted by God.

The Fulfillment of My Call

In 1998, I graduated from university with a bachelor's degree in government and a minor in English, but I had no idea what my future would hold. However, I had wanted to go on a mission trip. After searching the internet, which was still considered new at that time, I discovered Chosen People Ministries and decided to go on my first short-term mission. That volcano feeling went off in my gut again when I was accepted into their Summer Training and Evangelism Program (STEP). I went for training at Moody Bible Institute in Chicago, Illinois, followed by an evangelistic outreach on the streets of New York City. The daily worship and studying of God's word, followed by street evangelism and outreach, gave me such a love for reaching out to my people (the Jewish people) with the gospel of Yeshua. I experienced true joy as I saw people receiving the revelation and truth of our Messiah. That outreach totally rearranged my life's path.

For years, I had not appreciated my Messianic Jewish upbringing. I thought being Jewish wasn't an important part of my identity. I never forgot the call of God at Camp Cedar Crest, but I had also never realized how I would go into full-time ministry. After that mission trip, however, I knew that God had made me a Jew for a purpose: to reach my people and the nations as one of the redeemed of the House of Israel. So, to the utter shock of my parents, friends, and my church in Sacramento, I fully returned to my Jewish heritage and decided to study to become a Messianic rabbi.

At the end of the summer of 1998, I returned to southern California, the area of my childhood upbringing, and began studying both jewish and christian theology night and day over a three-year period. I traveled to Israel to see the land of my ancestors and to study in the actual places of the Bible. When I first landed in Israel at the beginning of my studies and my feet touched the ancient soil of my family, it was as if I had finally come home. It was there in Israel, the very place to which God had called Abraham to go, that I fell in deeper love with the Bible and redoubled my efforts to please God with my life.

The next year, I became the local youth pastor at Adat HaMashiach (a Messianic congregation) in Irvine, California. I loved my time serving that local community. I loved watching a young generation of Messianic believers choosing to follow the ways of God. It was fulfilling to be part of Adat HaMashiach, but deep down I was being drawn by God to look for more opportunities to further my spiritual journey.

I found a ministry and a mentor in Budapest, Hungary, and he had invited me to serve as an intern for a year before gaining the title of Messianic rabbi. I served there for over three years and was blessed to see many local Hungarians, Gypsies, and Jews (some were Holocaust survivors) come to faith in Yeshua. As an intern I helped lead youth camps in the former Soviet Union, train local believers, and help build new ministries. When I became a rabbi I had many additional responsibilities in leading the local congregation, presiding over weekly and special services (such as holidays, baptisms, and funerals), and the general day to day administration. I loved being a pastor and a missionary. Unfortunately, I loved the titles more than the work.

To be honest, I had no idea what I was doing in those early years. My mentor had taught me so much and given me so much responsibility that it felt good to be both praised and disciplined. I wanted to please my senior rabbi so much. Although it was the people-pleaser in me, my view of God was askew. My way to please God was by pleasing others. We would fast and pray every week, have constant training sessions, and start new ministries. I was always afraid that if we didn't do everything right, we would *miss* God's blessing, and in return, God would withhold His presence from us.

Everything had become so serious. I was only twenty-eight years old, but the Kingdom of God was no longer a place of joy. It had become more about the lost going to hell and God needing to be satisfied. At one point, I felt guilty for spending even half a day doing my laundry. I needed to do more and become better so God would be pleased. Even though I thought I had finally found what I was designed to do, there was one major thing lacking in my life: grace.

John 1:1-5

1 In the beginning was the Word, and the Word was with God, and the Word was God. 2 He was in the beginning with God. 3 All things were made through Him, and without Him nothing was made that was made.
4 In Him was life, and the life was the light of men.
5 And the light shines in the darkness, and the darkness did not comprehend it.

PART 2
Grace

The Revelation

When I was in Hungary, I had a revelation. Even though I had been serving in ministry since my teenage years, preaching God's word, and doing everything that I thought I should be doing, but when I looked into my heart of hearts, I felt as if something was missing.

According to *Merriam-Webster,* "grace" is defined as, "a virtue coming from God," and "a state of sanctification enjoyed through divine assistance." However, I had no idea what "virtue coming from God" or how I obtained "a state of sanctification enjoyed though divine assistance" meant.

The most important component of our faith—grace— was the greatest thing lacking in my life at that time. You may question how that could be possible, especially given my background. I was a man of faith, experience, and knowledge. Yeshua was my Lord. He was born of a virgin and lived a sinless life. I believed He was crucified for my sins and that He rose from the dead on the third day. I believed that He ascended to the Father, where He is waiting to return one day for us. Yet, to believe in Yeshua is not necessary to understand what He did for us, nor to realize the fullness of who God is.

Faith comes through a variety of ways, but revelation comes through the Holy Spirit. After receiving this message and revelation of the grace of God, my whole world started to unravel. It all began at a leadership retreat in Ukraine. As the associate rabbi of the congregation in Budapest, we were part of a network of Messianic congregations throughout the former Soviet Union. We would gather biannually for leadership training, fellowship, prayer, and encouragement. At that time, all the leaders from the congregations in our network were in the Crimea focusing on prayer, fasting, and getting a fresh word from God.

I remember sitting in the old retreat center. It was a comfortable evening and I was enjoying being with my many friends from all over the region. The Ukrainian pastor had a kind face and a gentle spirit. He stood before us and in his humility he captivated the room. Then it happened. A simple message on Matthew 18 about the unforgiving servant by a Ukrainian pastor about the truth of grace started the process of undoing me in such a profound way that my entire life would be changed. In my ministry, I wasn't known for being a man filled with grace. I was an excellent Bible teacher, I had many stories of the Holy Spirit's work in my life, I had been all over the world, but until that particular leadership retreat, I hadn't known about the gaping hole in my view of God. Prior to the retreat, I was a stern leader who was teaching others that the best way to serve God was to serve their leaders. I thought that being a rabbi was the highest of all callings. As a rabbi and missionary, I could please God by training others to sacrifice their families, their finances, and their time to follow God's vision for the congregation. In my stubbornness, I taught people that they would receive true acceptance by God if they served me and the goal of the congregation.

After that eventful encounter with God through the Ukrainian pastor's message, I returned to Budapest and my home congregation. I needed to meet with the leaders to ask their forgiveness for the mistakes I had made as their pastor. Because I had viewed God as a stern father who was always eager to judge me, I had been judging them. I realize now just how arrogant and prideful I had been, trying to make others please me in the same way that I was trying to please my leaders.

I first met with Stew and Millie, a couple who truly exuded the meekness of Yeshua. We met in a traditional European cafe. Sitting on small wooden chairs drinking very strong coffee and eating some Hungarian pastries, I wanted to bear my heart and ask forgiveness for my arrogance.

Before I had a chance to speak a word, the couple looked into my eyes and immediately asked, "Mathew, what has happened to you?"

With just one look, they could see that I had been profoundly changed. I was no longer the person I had been just four days earlier. It seems inconceivable that a person could be fundamentally changed in an instant, but that's what had happened to me.

So, what was the message that could profoundly change a person like myself? Let me try to unravel the concept that set me on a decade of transformation as a son of God. I will be grateful forever to that pastor in Ukraine for his faithfulness in sharing the message of grace.

Questions

God loves to speak to me in questions. God also likes to take me on a journey of discovery so that the truth of the Bible becomes a part of me. When I first began teaching in churches, conferences, and small groups I loved to teach all the knowledge I knew, whether I was living it out or not. Nowadays, I no longer teach theory or information, but everything I teach, share, or preach are all things that I have had to live out and implement in my own life. The topic of grace is the same. Many times in my life I had wondered— *Is God truly the same yesterday, today, and forever?*

When I was ten years old, I remember a particular day at a Vacation Bible School for children. The speaker had asked for volunteers to come forward. I didn't know what was going to be asked of us, but I did like getting the attention, so I quickly volunteered. I, along with a half-dozen other kids, stood on stage in front of our peers. There was a kiddie pool in the middle of the stage. We were asked to take off our socks and shoes. Then the speaker told us that we would each have a chance to walk on water. Murmurs spread throughout the crowd. I boldly walked up to the water, thinking of Peter, and stepped into the pool. Like all of the kids before me and after me, I was filled with great faith and hoped that a miracle would happen. But as I gently put my foot down, it crashed to the bottom of the pool.

Then the speaker proclaimed, "See! No one can walk on water. But back then, Jesus did."

I don't remember anything else that was said because I was distracted by the verse that was hanging on the wall of the sanctuary directly over the speaker's shoulder:

"Jesus Christ is the same yesterday, today and forever." (Hebrews 13:8)

I remember feeling so confused and thinking, *How dare this speaker say there was something we couldn't do that Yeshua did. He was the same, wasn't He?* Yeshua himself proclaimed that we would do greater things than He did in the Book of John. If we truly believe the Bible and what it says about God having no turning at all (James 1:17), then do we view the God of the Old Testament different from the God of the New Testament?

One time in Seoul, South Korea, I was asked this very question. I was sitting at a table with five or so young people in a cramped dessert cafe. Sunwoo, a twenty-something year old leader of the young people, asked me a question he had always struggled with: "Why does it appear there was one God of the Old Testament and a different one in the New Testament?" Every person at the table had the same question. My heart was broken as I realized that these young people had never been presented the truth about our God: He has never changed and never will change.

As a rabbi, one of my favorite things is to be asked questions. Many times, I don't answer questions directly but present stories or other questions that allow the asker to discover the answers for themselves. Sometimes we need to ponder questions for ourselves before being given the answer directly. Here are some questions about grace and God's character:

Can God live in the midst of sin?

Do you repent so you can be forgiven, or are you forgiven so you can repent?

When were you forgiven?

What is your personal understanding of sacrifice?

When did the Age of Grace begin?

What is the difference between grace and mercy?

What is the difference between judgment and grace?

How do we understand the cross and what Yeshua did and accomplished upon the cross?

Take a moment to think about your answers before reading on. If you like, write down a few sentences to answer each of these questions. Think about why you do what you do and which Scriptures you would use to back up those beliefs. As I begin to delve into the answers, we will have to look at history, culture, and our worldview to see what God actually did versus what most of us have been taught. I don't want to give the impression that what follows is a definitive exposé on grace. Instead, I hope this reflection on grace can be used as a means of inspiration as well as meditation.

Grace from the Beginning

There is a common dispensational belief that the Age of Grace began with the death and resurrection of Yeshua. The problem with this very simple statement is to imply that God did not have grace at first and then He did have grace. As I struggled with this concept, I needed to come to some conclusion. If God had always been a God of grace, then the Bible would have shown evidence of that. I asked God, "If you have always been the God of grace, please show me." The Lord asked me a simple question, "What was the first recorded sin in Genesis"? That was very easy: the first sin was committed by Adam and Eve in the Garden of Eden at the beginning of creation.

> Now the serpent was more cunning than any beast of the field which the Lord God had made. And he said to the woman, "Has God indeed said, 'You shall not eat of every tree of the garden?'"
> And the woman said to the serpent, "We may eat the fruit of the trees of the garden; but of the fruit of the tree which is in the midst of the garden, God has said, 'You shall not eat it, nor shall you touch it, lest you die.'"
> Then the serpent said to the woman, "You will not surely die. For God knows that in the day you eat of it your eyes will be opened, and you will be like God, knowing good and evil."
> So, when the woman saw that the tree was good for food, that it was pleasant to the eyes, and a tree desirable to make one wise, she took of its fruit and ate. She also gave to her husband with her, and he ate.

Then the eyes of both of them were opened, and they
knew that they were naked; and they sewed fig leaves
together and made themselves coverings.
(Genesis 3:1–7)

After Adam and Eve's sin, I began to think about what
followed. My thoughts concluded that God in His anger cursed
the serpent, Adam, and Eve, and even the land itself. Then, in
His wrath, God kicked Adam and Eve out from the garden. He
no longer allowed them to live in paradise. I thought of God as a
disappointed Father who had punished His sinful children. But
God interrupted my thinking and asked, "Then what happened?"
I realized that I needed to look again at the passages if God was
asking me this question.

And they heard the sound of the Lord God walking
in the garden in the cool of the day, and Adam and
his wife hid themselves from the presence of the Lord
God among the trees of the garden. (Genesis 3:8)

After reading this passage, I noticed something very
subtle that I had missed so many times before. It was the simple
phrase, "And they heard the sound of the Lord God walking…"
This hit me like a ton of bricks. I had always been taught that
God cannot dwell in the midst of sin and it was our sin that
had forever separated us from God. But it was so clear that God
had entered the Garden of Eden to spend time with Adam and
Eve even *after* they had sinned. Was He unaware of what had
happened? Did Adam and Eve somehow actually conceal what
they had done from God Himself? Yet even after sin had entered
the world, God did not leave His creation. He did not send His
angels to kick them out of Eden on His behalf or treat Adam

41

and Eve badly for their foolishness. God Himself entered the garden to converse with a now scared, frightened, and sinfully enlightened Adam and Eve.

Lessons from a Shepherd

In the Bible, God often refers to us as sheep. The Lord is our shepherd and He leads us to the still waters and makes us lay down in green pastures. There are also many lessons to learn as we embark on our spiritual journey. A true-life example comes from a dear Welsh friend of mine who lives in southwest Wales. He is an actual shepherd named Bob Gardner. Bob was in his seventies when he first had his revelation of who Yeshua was and gave his life to honor the Lord. Over the years, I have grown to love this man like a grandfather and to respect him as a man of great wisdom, strength, and godly character. I love to share many stories from Bob.

I try to learn from Bob, a real shepherd, about sheep whenever possible. One day, I was visiting Bob on the Bryntag Farm outside of Llanelli and he was excited to see me. He told me that he had waited all afternoon to show me how his sheep hear his voice. I was excited to be an up-close witness to a shepherd calling his sheep. As Bob walked out to the field, I noticed that the sheep stopped eating, walking, and even bleating. A wave of sheep heads lifted and watched in silence as Bob walked closer and closer to the field where they were grazing. After a few moments, Bob let out a call, and all the sheep immediately began to run to their shepherd. As he led them to a fresh pasture, they all followed him. It was truly amazing to witness hundreds of sheep following the call of their shepherd! Bob returned with a satisfied smile on his face. He told me that 423 sheep had changed pasture. This caught my attention because earlier Bob had said that there were 426 sheep in that particular field.

"What happened to the three other sheep?" I asked.

With a smile on his face and a gleam in his eye, Bob reported that three of the sheep were stuck in the bushes. "Do you know how stupid sheep are?" he asked.

I had learned something about the stupidity of sheep when I was studying in Israel, but I was confused and shook my head.

Bob continued, "Sheep are so stupid! When they are trapped in the bushes, they literally can scare themselves to death. Once a sheep gets stuck, there's no way it can free itself. As I approach to rescue them, they become even more frightened even though they know I am their shepherd. The sheep become so scared that they will push themselves further into the bushes to flee from me. In their frenzy to get away, they can actually impale themselves on the branches. I have to use my shepherd's crook to hold them still so they won't kill themselves. When they have calmed down, I firmly grab their fleece and lift them out of the bramble."

Bob's sheep behaved exactly the same way as Adam and Eve did in the garden. After sinning they tried to hide from the approaching Shepherd. But God did not leave His creation to die alone in their sin. Instead, God drew near to them to rescue them and deliver them from their folly. Therefore, we can learn that one of the first principles of grace is that our sin does not cause God to flee from us, but it causes God to *pursue* us. However, when we sin, we try to flee from God even if it means to our death. It is the Shepherd's responsibility to pursue His lost sheep and prevent us from killing ourselves.

A True Look at the Ramifications of Sin

When God finally did call Adam and Eve into the light, I began to see a very different God. He wasn't the angry "get out of my sight" God, but rather a teacher who took the time to inform them of their error and the consequences of their sin. He was the "I am pursuing you in the midst of the most foolish thing you have ever done" God. He was the true Father of His children, disciplining those whom He loves.

When Adam and Eve lived in the Garden of Eden, they never needed to worry about what to do. When everything you do is correct, you don't need to worry about it. But after sin had entered the world, and with it the understanding of the knowledge of "good and evil," Adam and Eve needed to learn that there were going to be consequences from sinning. They were about to learn what would be reaped from sowing sin into their lives: death, hard work because the earth would no longer yield freely, pain in child birth, but also hope for their foolishness. After the first sin, God released the first prophecy of the coming Messiah:

> So, the Lord God said to the serpent: "Because you have done this, you are cursed more than all cattle, and more than every beast of the field; on your belly you shall go, and you shall eat dust all the days of your life. And I will put enmity between you and the woman, and between your seed and her Seed; He shall bruise your head, and you shall bruise His heel." (Genesis 3:14–15 NKJV)

Our amazing God witnessed His beloved creation bring sin into the world and forever change the destiny of all mankind.

Yet He did not react out of anger, spite, or disappointment, but instead drew near to Adam and Eve. He brought correction to them, informed them of the hardships to come, but also released hope to all the world in the coming seed, which would stomp on the head of the cunning serpent. For it would be Yeshua who would be the seed of Eve that would trample on the head of the serpent, bringing eternal hope back to a fallen world. That was how our God responded to the very first sin.

Several years ago, my parents' neighbor, Terry, had become sick with cancer. It was a very sad time when he passed away. My mom took his death very hard. One day, as my mother drove past her neighbor's house, she felt a great sadness that Terry was no longer there in his home. While driving, she cried out to the Lord, "God, I really miss Terry being there." She wasn't expecting a response, but the Lord said, "That's how I felt when you weren't in the garden any longer. I miss you being there." God didn't say to my mother that He *only* missed Adam and Eve in the garden. To this day, God misses us living in the garden where we were meant to dwell. He feels sadness and loss that we cannot live in the garden with Him while He chooses to live in a fallen world with us.

My mom's story highlighted to me the heart of our true friend and God. The ramifications of the first sin were so profound because God also suffers the loss with us. He created us for a relationship and we damaged that relationship, but God has always been pursuing us to fix what was broken. God isn't a disappointed, angry, and wrathful God, but rather a heartbroken friend. I truly believe we need to continuously grasp how very different and higher God's ways are than ours.

The Second Sin

Many people have been taught to believe that God in the Old Testament is an angry God, but as you can see, God loves us, cares for us, and this has always been consistent. It is always important to keep an open mind, especially when it involves things that we believe deep in our core. My revelation of how God reacted after Adam and Eve sinned wouldn't have been possible if I hadn't looked deep into my own faith and recognized that something was missing.

God continued making His point, so one day He asked me, "What was the next recorded sin after Adam and Eve?"

That question seemed simple. "The second sin was when Cain killed his brother Abel," I said. God then told me to read the story again. As I reread Genesis chapter 4, I was struck by the fact that God was speaking directly with Cain, as would a friend, mentor, or father. And Cain was not surprised to be talking with God.

God warned Cain of the crouching sin waiting to strike. We know that Cain ultimately killed his brother. God sought out Cain and asked where his brother was. Then Cain infamously responded, "Am I my brother's keeper?" We know that Cain's sin was easily discovered. The blood of Abel was crying out to God from the ground. God then told Cain, as He had told his parents before him, the consequences of his actions. It is remarkable that God didn't call for the stoning of Cain or for his execution. Instead, God proclaimed:

> "So now you are cursed from the earth, which has
> opened its mouth to receive your brother's blood
> from your hand. When you till the ground, it shall

no longer yield its strength to you. A fugitive and a
vagabond you shall be on the earth."
(Genesis 4:11–12)

Cain's response was not to apologize or plead for
forgiveness. Rather he called upon the mercy of God. He cried out
to the Lord that his punishment was too much and that whoever
would find him would kill him. God responded yet again:

And the Lord said to him, "Therefore, whoever kills
Cain, vengeance shall be taken on him sevenfold."
And the Lord set a mark on Cain, lest anyone finding
him should kill him. (Genesis 4:15)

I had always thought of the Lord's mark on Cain as a
branding of shame. I thought the mark represented God's
humiliation because of Cain's sin, but instead the word used in
Hebrew אות (*ot*) is the same word used to show the sign of a
covenant. God's reaction to Cain's sin of the murder of his own
brother was to make an everlasting covenant with him, to protect
him. Later, God replaced the line of Abel by giving Adam and
Eve another son named Seth.

In this encounter, it amazes me that God forgave Cain
and granted him both grace and mercy without *any* sign of
repentance, asking for forgiveness, or even a sacrifice. God also
went above and beyond by restoring the sin of Cain through
the birth of Seth. What an amazing God! He draws near in the
moment of a man's worst sin, hears him, talks with him, and even
begins the process of restoring him.

A Man after God's Heart

The first two examples of sin that the earth bore witness to have been recorded to demonstrate the foundational character of our God. Our God pursues, brings conviction not condemnation, releases, empowers, communicates, makes a covenant, and forgives. He dwells with us and gives hope to those who have done the wrong. If our God has not changed, then we can be assured that He acts in the same way today as He did for Adam, Eve, or even Cain. The examples of His grace continue right through the entire Torah, the Prophets, and the other writings of the Bible.

One of the greatest heroes of the Bible is King David. It is very easy for us to romanticize a figure in the Bible, especially our heroes, but we must view them for who they are. David was the youngest in his family line and the most insignificant. He was placed in the role of a lonely shepherd while his brothers were away serving King Saul in Israel's army. He was born at a time when Israel had done the very thing Moses had warned them not to do: They had chosen a king. King Saul was the peoples' king and a man who exposed their hearts. David, on the other hand, was a man through whom God would reveal His grace, mercy, and majesty.

Under instruction from God, the prophet Samuel went to look for the young shepherd boy in Bethlehem. Samuel did not expect to look for the youngest. After meeting all seven of Jesse's older sons, the prophet asked if there was yet another. The Lord had not chosen any of the seven. Only when the youngest and smallest, with a ruddy complexion (an apparent disadvantage) appeared before him, did God have Samuel anoint David to be the future king of Israel.

God spoke of David as a man after His own heart. However, we know that David had many shortcomings as a man. His children did vile, unspeakable things from rape to murder. David was also a man of great lust and lusted after Bathsheba from his rooftop in Jerusalem while she was immersing in a ritual bath. After he had sex with her, he lied, manipulated, and eventually murdered her husband Uriah to keep his sin secret. However, Bathsheba was pregnant with David's child. So, after the birth, the Lord commanded the child to die. Even as God's anointed, there are consequences to our sins, which may still produce death. I can't imagine having to deal with the guilt, shame, and powerlessness of these kinds of consequences. For certain, David would have concluded that because of his sin, God would cast him away. However, God's heart for David had never changed. Even before David had done any of the sinful and distasteful acts of evil, which God knew about beforehand, God had declared David to be a man after His own heart.

Our God, who knew David's future, did not withhold any of His blessings, promises, or relationship ties because of past, present, or future sin. Regardless of God's knowledge of David's sins, God never took David's crown away. God never disowned him, never cast him aside, and never removed the Holy Spirit from him. Instead, God not only forgave David repeatedly, He made a Covenant of Salt and promised that his descendants after him would be the kings of Israel forever. A Covenant of Salt was the second most difficult covenant to break in biblical times. It was called a Covenant of Salt because after the covenantal agreement was made, salt was cast into the wind. If a person, or in this case God, wanted to change or break the terms of the covenant, He would have had to find and return every grain of salt.

David had a destiny. God had called him to be a righteous

king. Because of his faith, he was that. David's greatest desire was to build God's House so that all of Israel would be able to come and worship together. However, there was blood on David's hands as consequences from his sin, so he was prohibited from completing his dream. God's heart for David was so great and David's understanding of God's heart was so immense that even after being blocked from building God's House, David did not feel rejected by God. Instead, he rejoiced that God would allow the Temple to be built by his son, Solomon (the promised child of redemption between David and Bathsheba), who became Israel's second righteous king. God continued to honor David, an imperfect person, as a monarch.

All of us have fought the genuine fear that our sins disqualify us from serving God. We have feared that our sins would prevent us from having a good relationship with Him. We must overcome the fear that God would reject us or leave us. You may ask, "What about David's psalm that asks God to not cast him away?":

"Create in me a clean heart, O God,
And renew a steadfast spirit within me.
Do not cast me away from Your presence,
And do not take Your Holy Spirit from me."
(Psalm 51:10–11)

This is a beautiful psalm and sung in many churches. I believe this psalm was portraying the genuine fear that David had about not receiving God's love because of his sins, written after some of his greatest transgressions. Even though David wrote about his fear and his feelings doesn't make it a biblical doctrine. We should not enter into the same deception, fear, or doubt that David had since we have a fuller truth, a greater revelation. We live in the day of the fullness of promise and the Bible. To gain this faith and reassurance we must then look to David's future descendant: Yeshua.

Isaiah 9:6-7

6 For unto us a Child is born,
Unto us a Son is given;
And the government will be upon His shoulder.
And His name will be called
Wonderful, Counselor, Mighty God,
Everlasting Father, Prince of Peace.
7 Of the increase of His government and peace
There will be no end,
Upon the throne of David and over His kingdom,
To order it and establish it with judgment and justice
From that time forward, even forever.
The zeal of the Lord of hosts will perform this.

PART 3
Yeshua (Jesus)

The Good News in Capernaum

The New Testament begins with the Gospels proclaiming the Good News. There is no greater news than to see how Yeshua dealt with the forgiveness of our sin and the issue of repentance. In one of the first ministry moments in Capernaum, on the Sea of Galilee, Yeshua was teaching inside the house of Peter's mother-in-law. Many gathered together and filled the house overflowing, as everyone in the village wanted to hear Yeshua. Some industrious men, who were desperate to see Him, climbed up on the top of the roof, broke through it, and lowered a paralyzed man to the feet of Yeshua.

As the paralytic man lay in front of Jesus, everyone waited with bated breath to see what Yeshua would do.

When Jesus saw their faith,
He said to the paralytic, "Son, your sins are forgiven you." (Mark 2:5)

Everyone present would have been shocked at such a public declaration.

And some of the scribes were sitting there and
reasoning in their hearts,
"Why does this Man speak blasphemies like this?
Who can forgive sins but God alone?" (Mark 2:6–7)

If we believe that Yeshua is the Messiah and the Son of God, we would think, *Yeshua is God, so of course He can forgive sin*. But it must be noted that at this point in Yeshua's ministry, He is only a man, having laid down His Godhead. Therefore, living as a man, Yeshua operated only with the authority of Adam, the same authority (in this context, authority is the right to forgive sins, preach the good news, and to perform miracles) God gave every man and woman upon their birth. As Paul wrote:

> Let this mind be in you which was also in Christ
> Jesus, who, being in the form of God, did not
> consider it robbery to be equal with God, but made
> Himself of no reputation, taking the form of a
> bondservant, and coming in the likeness of men.
> (Philippians 2:5–7)

Since Yeshua never sinned, He never lost His authority as a man (the authority given through Adam). The truth is that Yeshua wasn't some god-man hybrid like Hercules or some other pagan deity. He was a true Son doing the work of His Father. He had told His own parents in Jerusalem when He was just a young boy, "I am about my Father's business" (Luke 2:49). Yeshua responded to the internal conflict and public shock to His statement in Capernaum:

> But immediately, when Jesus perceived in His spirit
> that they reasoned thus within themselves, He said to
> them, "Why do you reason about these things in your
> hearts? Which is easier, to say to the paralytic, 'Your
> sins are forgiven you,' or to say, 'arise, take up your
> bed and walk?' But that you may know that the Son
> of Man has power on earth to forgive sins"— He said
> to the paralytic, "I say to you, arise, take up your bed,
> and go to your house." (Mark 2:8–11)

Yeshua simply told the paralyzed man to take up his bed

and walk. There is no record of the man asking for forgiveness. He had not offered a sacrifice to God that we know of. There's no proof that he was sorry for any of his sins. Yet, the man's sins were forgiven at that very moment because of one simple principle: the "Kingdom of God" is about the "Will of Heaven," forgiveness, and the releasing of sin.

> In this manner, therefore, pray:
> Our Father in heaven,
> Hallowed be Your name.
> Your kingdom come.
> Your will be done
> On earth as it is in heaven.
> Give us this day our daily bread.
> And forgive us our sins,
> As we forgive those who have sinned against us.
> (Matthew 6:9–12)

Yeshua showed us in the Lord's Prayer that the key principle of His Father's Kingdom and God's will in heaven to be done on Earth is all about forgiveness and the flowing of grace. Yeshua walked fully in His Father's will on the earth. He was the perfect man accomplishing the work that Adam could not, to give all of us hope for the impossible and indisputable truth about the love of God.

Grace versus Judgment

A second story that powerfully demonstrates Yeshua living out the principle of God's Kingdom and the will of heaven can be found in John chapter 8. It is the story of the woman caught in the act of adultery. In the cultural context of the story she was being accused of being a prostitute. The woman was guilty of sin and was brought to the Temple for justice. Don't get distracted about who brought the woman and why the man, who had been caught with her, wasn't also brought to the Temple for justice. Instead, it's important to realize that this woman was fully and completely guilty of her actions. This woman, who lived just a short distance from the very House of God in the city of God, Jerusalem, brought a curse upon the land by sinning against God and herself through her sexual lifestyle. Her actions were worthy of death according to the Torah. Therefore, she could have been put to death justifiably. What took place next was something that shook the very foundations of their faith.

As was Yeshua's custom, He was in the Temple (His Father's house) teaching. It was just after one of the three great pilgrimage feasts in which all Jewish men, who were able, would have presented themselves before God at the Temple, according to Exodus:

> "Three times you shall keep a feast to Me in the year: You shall keep the Feast of Unleavened Bread (you shall eat unleavened bread seven days, as I commanded you, at the time appointed in the month of Aviv, for in it you came out of Egypt; none shall appear before Me empty); and the Feast of Harvest [also known as the Feast of Weeks or Pentecost], the first fruits of your labors which you have sown in the field; and the Feast of Ingathering [also known as the Feast of Tabernacles or Feast of Booths] at the end of the year, when you have gathered in the fruit of your labors from the field. Three times in the year all your

males shall appear before the Lord God."
(Exodus 23:14–17)

The Feast of Tabernacles has many meanings, but one of the most powerful ones is that it is the season of Immanuel (God, with us). The feast commemorates God's faithfulness to the Israelites through the desert years and into the Promised Land. It was a time of giving to the Lord of the people's tithes and offerings, acknowledging that all things come from Him. It was a time of great blessing and teaching for all who attended the feast. Yeshua was a featured teacher during this season, and as we know, He was not afraid of creating controversy. During the feast, Yeshua had once again caused a great stir and commotion in Jerusalem. This incensed the religious authorities and the power players of the city to discredit Him. The religious leaders orchestrated the event of bringing the adulterous woman to the feet of Yeshua in order to trap him in front of all the people. First came the accusation; then came the setting of the trap.

"Teacher, this woman was caught in adultery, in the very act. Now Moses, in the law, commanded us that such should be stoned. But what do You say?"
(John 8:4–5)

This type of scheme was a clever but normal type of confrontation and accusation, especially when sin was being made public by a religious institution. It was the design of using shame, humiliation, isolation, and condemnation to gather the people to your side, for fear of their own sin being revealed. Even today it is a common tactic to force someone to react in a specific way. Yeshua did not take the bait. Instead, He did something totally unexpected. In verse 6, Yeshua pretends He never heard the men and begins to draw on the ground with His finger.

> This they said, testing Him, that they might have
> something of which to accuse Him. But Jesus stooped
> down and wrote on the ground with His finger, as
> though He did not hear. (John 8:6)

Over the years, there have been many theories about what Yeshua wrote on the ground. Did He list the names of the accusers, or did He simply write the sins of those who stood before Him? Nobody knows what was written because the Bible doesn't record that information. One thing we can know about our God: *He never humiliates us nor condemns us... never!*

God would not publicly behave in the same spirit as the men who were now trying to trap Yeshua. God does not operate with the desire to distort, dishonor, or bring shame upon the very creation that bears His image. Whatever Yeshua wrote in the dirt, I believe that in the silence He created space to bring true conviction of the Holy Spirit—not just for the woman or her accusers, but also for the disciples, the regular listeners at the Temple, the visitors, and those who would have gathered in curiosity. At that moment, everyone was about to learn one of the greatest principles of heaven.

After writing on the ground and infuriating the plans of the religious leaders of Jerusalem, they kept pressing Yeshua to answer:

> So, when they continued asking Him, He raised
> Himself up and said to them, "He who is without sin
> among you, let him throw a stone at her first."
> (John 8:7)

The story continues with Yeshua stooping down to write once again. Then, from the oldest to the last, each person was convicted of his own sin and left. But imagine if they had stayed. It was a very public and open space, and all of the bystanders would have watched and listened to what would happen next. It must be noted again that the woman's sin was very real; she was guilty and culturally reviled. The result of her actions should have been corporal punishment. But the only person who was qualified to throw the first stone was Yeshua, who had no sin.

There, on the mountain of God, a sinless, perfect Yeshua who had just taught in His Father's house, was about to pass judgment, not just upon this woman but upon all of Israel. This is a mirrored reflection of the book of Hosea, where God calls Israel a harlot.

> Do not rejoice, Oh Israel, with joy like other peoples,
> for you have played the harlot against your God.
> You have made love for hire on every threshing floor.
> (Hosea 9:1)

The woman, who sat before Yeshua, was a prophetic symbol of all of Israel. Yet, like all of Israel, her immediate fate now rested in the hands of the sinless and perfect Yeshua.

> When Jesus had raised Himself up and saw no one
> but the woman, He said to her, "Woman, where
> are those accusers of yours? Has no one condemned
> you?" (John 8:10)

Just like when God questioned Adam and Eve in the Garden of Eden or Cain in the field, He now questioned the prostitute and already knew the answer. He knew her sin; He knew her guilt. We must remember that all of the people who were standing and listening as witnesses to this happening had never seen or heard anything like this before. The adulterous woman who stood there in the midst of everyone, guilty and exposed, answered:

She said, "No one, Lord." (John 8:11a)

Notice that she did not fall to His feet in supplication. There was no crying recorded. We do not read of groveling or begging for mercy. The woman knew she didn't deserve any of it. She was guilty, humiliated, and unmasked before the whole Jewish community. This wretched woman was standing in the House of the Lord, where she had no right to be, guilty as charged. She was unclean physically, emotionally, and spiritually.

Jesus answered to her, "Neither do I condemn you; go and sin no more." (John 8:11b)

How could this be? How could Yeshua extend mercy and grace to her? She did not deserve it and could never have paid for it. Yet, Yeshua said to her, "Neither do I condemn you."

A definition for "mercy" is to be brought into a right relationship with God. "Grace" could be defined as being given the ability to stay in a relationship with God. When Yeshua referred to her as "woman," this was not in a chauvinistic or derogatory use of the word for a nameless person before Him. Instead, it was what God had called Eve when He first created her. "Woman," wonderfully and perfectly made. Yeshua restored her true identity as God had originally designed in the garden. Then, Yeshua forgave the woman and released her sin and guilt, bringing her into a relationship with God in His own house.

Yeshua taught the woman, us, and Israel God's ways. He showed us how to make disciples, how to make peace, and how to allow the "Kingdom to come" and "will to be done" on Earth as it is in heaven.

In the House of the Lord and at the conclusion of the Feast of Tabernacles, Yeshua was sitting in authority as a prophetic fulfillment of the Scriptures. It was a literal fulfillment of David's psalm and prophecies found in both Isaiah and Micah:

"I was glad when they said to me,
'Let us go into the house of the Lord.'" (Psalm 122)

Many people/nations shall come and say,
"Come, and let us go up to the mountain of the Lord,
To the house of the God of Jacob;
He will teach us His ways,
And we shall walk in His paths."
For out of Zion shall go forth the law,
And the word of the Lord from Jerusalem.
(Isaiah 2:3/Micah 4:2)

We are always trying to think of justice and mercy as a set of balancing scales, but this is not the Kingdom of God with justice in one hand and mercy in the other. The highest form of God's judgment, the highest law in God's kingdom, is grace. The law that went forth from Zion to Israel and all the nations was the law of grace and mercy.

Schadenfreude

I grew up in the church in America, and occasionally there would be news of fallen leaders and high-profile people who had committed immoral sins. Some churches were swift to expose, condemn, fire, or remove those leaders from their positions. There would be pictures of crying evangelists and pastors, which brought media controversies about sin and how the churches dealt with them. The organizations I was a member of and ministered in were just as swift and public. I was taught by a leader that it was better to judge each other harshly now with our sin so it wouldn't be as bad when God showed up. There was hardly any safety, freedom, or expressions of grace extended. To be a follower of Yeshua meant swift, unyielding justice to followers who trampled on biblical moirés.

Once, while I was at university, we had a major week of evangelism on campus. One afternoon, I was in the main quad when my friends and I took part in a preplanned skit to drum up curiosity that would lead to an evangelist-led discussion with students who were interested. My friend threw a woman to the ground and pretended to kick her. We shouted at her and called her names to reenact the passage of John 8. I always loved drama and enthusiastically got into the part.

People all around came to see what the disturbance was. Many people laughed, some even got into it by shouting obscenities at her, while a few had concerned looks on their faces, wondering if we were really mistreating this girl. Looking back at it now, I realize that I oddly enjoyed being the one who exposed the adulterous woman publicly.

It was liberating to get the attention, but deep down, I realize that I was living out my own worldview of how I felt God would deal with me. I was morbidly afraid that God would expose my own secret sin. I believed that if I could demonstrate how holy I was, then maybe, just maybe, God would not expose me. By my own holiness, I was faithfully involved with evangelism on my university campus, participated in as many church meetings as possible, and I never missed a prayer meeting.

It's interesting that God wasn't the one who publicly exposed the woman in John 8, the preacher on TV, or myself. However, we are the ones who expose and tear down others to make ourselves feel better. There's even a psychological term for it: "*Schadenfreude*," "the pleasure we take in the misfortune of others, either physically, emotional or spiritually." Our inner desire or fear wants us to be holy and righteous. I loved it when another preacher fell or a high-profile leader was exposed because my view of a disciplinarian God was thus reaffirmed.

In hindsight, my university performance in the skit was an exposure of myself as a religious hypocrite because I did not understand how God forgave, released, reaffirmed, or renewed the adulterous woman. I was acting out a false image of God. I was reinforcing a fear of a God who delighted in publicly revealing hidden sin. Secretly, I was terrified that because of my private sin, God would remove me from His presence and determine I was not worthy of His affection or sacrifice. I did not understand the God of grace.

Psalm 22

The Suffering, Praise, and Posterity of the Messiah
To the Chief Musician. Set to "The Deer of the Dawn." A Psalm of David.

1 My God, My God, why have You forsaken Me?
Why are You so far from helping Me,
And from the words of My groaning?
2 O My God, I cry in the daytime, but You do not hear;
And in the night season, and am not silent.
3 But You are holy,
Enthroned in the praises of Israel.
4 Our fathers trusted in You;
They trusted, and You delivered them.
5 They cried to You, and were delivered;
They trusted in You, and were not ashamed.
6 But I am a worm, and no man;
A reproach of men, and despised by the people.
7 All those who see Me ridicule Me;
They shoot out the lip, they shake the head, saying,
8 "He trusted in the Lord, let Him rescue Him;
Let Him deliver Him, since He delights in Him!"
9 But You are He who took Me out of the womb;
You made Me trust while on My mother's breasts.
10 I was cast upon You from birth.
From My mother's womb
You have been My God.
11 Be not far from Me,
For trouble is near;
For there is none to help.
12 Many bulls have surrounded Me;
Strong bulls of Bashan have encircled Me.
13 They gape at Me with their mouths,
Like a raging and roaring lion.
14 I am poured out like water,
And all My bones are out of joint;
My heart is like wax;
It has melted within Me.
15 My strength is dried up like a potsherd,
And My tongue clings to My jaws;
You have brought Me to the dust of death.
16 For dogs have surrounded Me;
The congregation of the wicked has enclosed Me.
They pierced My hands and My feet;
17 I can count all My bones.
They look and stare at Me.

18 They divide My garments among them,
And for My clothing they cast lots.
19 But You, O Lord, do not be far from Me;
O My Strength, hasten to help Me!
20 Deliver Me from the sword,
My precious life from the power of the dog.
21 Save Me from the lion's mouth
And from the horns of the wild oxen!
You have answered Me.
22 I will declare Your name to My brethren;
In the midst of the assembly I will praise You.
23 You who fear the Lord, praise Him!
All you descendants of Jacob, glorify Him,
And fear Him, all you offspring of Israel!
24 For He has not despised nor abhorred the affliction of the
afflicted;
Nor has He hidden His face from Him;
But when He cried to Him, He heard.
25 My praise shall be of You in the great assembly;
I will pay My vows before those who fear Him.
26 The poor shall eat and be satisfied;
Those who seek Him will praise the Lord.
Let your heart live forever!
27 All the ends of the world
Shall remember and turn to the Lord,
And all the families of the nations
Shall worship before You.
28 For the kingdom is the Lord's,
And He rules over the nations.
29 All the prosperous of the earth
Shall eat and worship;
All those who go down to the dust
Shall bow before Him,
Even he who cannot keep himself alive.
30 A posterity shall serve Him.
It will be recounted of the Lord to the next generation,
31 They will come and declare His righteousness to a people
who will be born,
That He has done this.

PART 4
Yeshua (Jesus) Means Salvation

Grace and Sacrifice

In the past, I have been overwhelmed with the guilt of my continued sin. I used to want nothing more than to hide my face and run away from God. I used to think, *How could I be worthy to receive the sacrifice of Yeshua?* Even crucifixes were a constant reminder of the pain that Yeshua suffered because of our iniquities.

From Sunday school through university, I was taught that Yeshua died on the cross because of our sin. I was taught that I was partly responsible for Yeshua's death. Each person, as a sinner, needed to take his or her own responsibility for crucifying Yeshua. Personally, I felt guilty for Yeshua having to go to the cross. I felt I was causing Him to be whipped, tortured, humiliated, ridiculed, and ultimately sacrificed in such a horrific way.

Many people have seen the movie, *The Passion of the Christ,* which portrayed in graphic detail the brutalization and crucifixion of Yeshua. I remember reading an article on *The Passion of the Christ* official web site where Mel Gibson said that the scene of the Roman soldier's hands hammering the nails into Yeshua were intentionally his own to be symbolic of the fact that he holds himself accountable for the Messiah's death. Many of us feel the same way. When we see the faceless hands lift the hammer up and down, we imagine that it was our sin and our hands that sacrificed the Savior.

Sacrifices were burdens that I could never live up to. It seemed that the laying down, the high cost, and the ritual offerings were too much. I had only guilt that Yeshua had become a sacrifice for me. I never had the right mindset of what the term "sacrifice" truly meant. Most of my Christian concepts came from attending a traditional church as a child. It wasn't until I began my rabbinical studies that I saw the profound differences between the traditional Christian view and that of the Jewish people.

After asking hundreds of evangelical Christians over the years of how they would define "sacrifice" and my extensive internet searches on the topic, I have noted similar types of answers. The most common words and phrases were: *to lay down, to let go, to cost something, pain, suffering, love, to pay a price, blood, atonement, endure, suffer, and forgo or give up something you don't want to give up.*

For the Jewish people, "sacrifice" means something very different, so I needed to reconcile these different views. Had I been the cause of Yeshua's pain, suffering, and sacrifice, then I would have known I was guilty and would never have been worthy of the sacrifice He offered for me. Instead, I would have always tried to live up to or earn His gift, hoping that I would someday feel worthy enough to accept what He had done for me on the cross.

Guilt and Shame

The truth is we can never live up to a mindset built on guilt and shame. The guilt of the sacrifice of Yeshua has been used throughout the ages as a means of controlling people's behavior. It was used to enforce authority and the preeminence of the institution of the organized church.

For example, the sermon about Yeshua's last night on Earth is still being used to drum up guilt and shame. After Yeshua had had His final Passover meal with His disciples (The Lord's Supper) and had sent Judas away to quickly go and do what he had intended, the remaining disciples followed Him to the

Garden of Gethsemane. In the garden, Yeshua went to a quiet place to pray before He was eventually betrayed by Judas and then arrested. This night is often referred to as the dark night of Yeshua.

At this very location in Israel there now stands the Church of all Nations. Inside this humble church, open to all denominations of Christianity, is a perpetual memorial to that night. As you enter in silence, the dark purple stained-glass windows shade the interior, always capturing the last night of Yeshua. The gospels of Mark and Luke give an account of this particular event. In the garden, Yeshua prayed:

"Father, if it is Your will, take this cup away from Me; Nevertheless, not My will, but Yours, be done."
(Luke 22:24)

This verse was always a huge burden to me. It demonstrated my warped belief that Yeshua wanted to get out of going to the cross. Would you choose to endure the pain, the suffering, and the humiliation that was about to ensue? As Yeshua prayed in the darkness, with the weight of all eternity upon His shoulders, He asked His Father to "take this cup away from Me." Yet, in obedience, Yeshua did the will of His Father and drank the cup of suffering. He didn't want to suffer, but He had to because of our collective sin. Therefore, every time I sinned, I felt like I was personally rubbing salt in Yeshua's wounds.

As a pastor, rabbi, and missionary, I have taken part in a repentance service known as a "Come to the Cross Service." It was customary to use the Garden of Gethsemane story first followed by a message about sin and repentance that was accompanied by the video of the brutal crucifixion of Yeshua. We thought this was the best way to get young people to feel the guilt, shame, and weight of their sin so that they would repent and see the need for a Savior. We would then give an altar call. We would ask all those who wanted to accept Yeshua into their hearts for the first time or wanted to rededicate themselves to the Lord to come forward. Nearly every single person would come and kneel before the cross, very distraught with tears in their eyes. Some came forward out of genuine revelation. Many came out of shame, guilt, and remorse. Some came out of peer pressure.

Though I was trained to lead these kinds of services, after my transformation in Ukraine, something began to bother me. It didn't feel right. I wasn't sure why I no longer liked using the Garden of Gethsemane story as a way to levy guilt upon people. I struggled with the idea of Yeshua not wanting to go through with the crucifixion. Then, I started studying all of the gospel accounts surrounding and leading up to the crucifixion. After reading the happenings in context, my former teachings no longer made sense. For example, just a few weeks before that night in the Garden of Gethsemane, Yeshua told His disciples that He was going to Jerusalem to die. He also told the disciples not to worry, for He was willing to lay down His life because He had been given the authority to take it up again.

> "Therefore, My Father loves Me, because I lay down
> My life that I may take it again. No one takes it from
> Me, but I lay it down of Myself. I have power to
> lay it down, and I have power to take it again. This
> command I have received from My Father."
> (John 10:17–18)

Then He commanded His disciples that they should tell no one that He was Jesus the Christ. From that time Jesus began to show to His disciples that He

must go to Jerusalem, and suffer many things from
the elders and chief priests and scribes, and be killed,
and be raised the third day. (Matthew 16:20–21)

After years of searching, reading and studying, I came
upon a Jewish teacher in Israel who was teaching on covenantal
and ancient Jewish rituals. What transpired there opened my eyes.
This teaching helped give me a new context for what actually
happened that night in the Garden of Gethsemane. It filled me
with such wonderment, I had to weep. When the events in the
Garden of Gethsemane were taken in context, in all four gospels,
and with a little knowledge of the past, I gained a revelation of
what Yeshua did that changed how I would teach about the cross.

The Garden of Gethsemane Story Explained

How many times have we been told that it was our sin
that placed Yeshua upon the cross? Personally, I had struggled
with accepting Yeshua's sacrifice because I never felt worthy of it.
We need to learn the difference between the traditional Christian
and Jewish view of "sacrifice."

The word "sacrifice," defined by the *Oxford Dictionary*
reveals the following:
"an act of slaughtering an animal or person, or
surrendering a possession as an offering to God, or to
a divine or supernatural figure."

Synonyms: a ritual slaughter, offering, oblation,
immolation
"the sacrifice of animals"

- an animal, person, or object offered in a sacrifice.
  synonyms: (votive) offering, burnt offering,
  gift, oblation "the calf was a sacrifice"
- an act of giving up something valued for the
  sake of something else regarded as more important or
  worthy "we must all be prepared to make sacrifices"
  synonyms: surrender, giving up,
  abandonment, renunciation, forfeiture,
  relinquishment, resignation, abdication

This general definition of "sacrifice" mirrors the typical Christian understanding. But for Jewish people, "sacrifice" is viewed very differently. Born out of our history through the Torah and the Prophets, we are able to gain a deeper implication of sacrifice. *Simply stated, sacrifice can be defined as a means to stay in or return to a relationship with the Almighty.* The primary synonym for "sacrifice" would be "relationship."

Ancient Israel performed their sacrifices to remain in a relationship with God. The sacrifices were not thought of in terms of their cost or the giving up of things. A sacrifice was to be thought of in terms of thanksgiving and rejoicing because the sacrifice gave the believers in God a way to reconcile their broken relationships with God. All sacrifices had to be freewill offerings, given with a joyful heart, and could not be done with an ulterior motive. The requirements by God for sacrifices are laid out in the book of Leviticus chapters 1–7, 19 and 22.

So, if Yeshua was not willing, was not joyful, and had not chosen to go to the cross freely, then His death as a sacrifice would not have been acceptable before God the Father. If we look at the offering and sacrifice of Yeshua with a biblical Jewish understanding of relationship, we will learn our cultural context for the Garden of Gethsemane conversation between Yeshua and

His Father and see a much different story unfold. As I learned about the ancient Jewish rituals and covenantal practices, I discovered that Yeshua's prayer, "O My Father, if it is possible, let this cup pass before Me; nevertheless, not as I will, as You will." (Matthew 26:39) was not a prayer of desperation asking God to allow Yeshua to get out of going to the cross. Instead, Yeshua was demonstrating a wedding betrothal ritual between Himself and all mankind.

When a man and a woman were arranged to be married, their families had to follow several stages for the engagement. The first stage would be the creation of a marriage contract. This contract was called a *ketubah*. Jews still use them to this day. My parents have theirs hanging on the living room wall. A ketubah lists the responsibilities of the groom toward the bride and it is signed by witnesses. But if either the groom or bride become unfaithful prior to the wedding, then the contract could be torn up without having to consummate the wedding.

The second level of the engagement was to discuss the bridal price. After the bride's price was agreed upon and ultimately paid, the couple would become betrothed. Once betrothal had taken place, the groom and bride were required to follow through with the marriage. The only way to not consummate the wedding would have been for the couple to have gotten an official divorce.

Many people in the world today come from broken families and understand the painful realities of divorce. Because of this, it is easy to believe that God could indeed want a divorce when a spouse is unfaithful. However, in the book of Hosea, we see an amazing depiction of God's nature through a prophet who was instructed by God to marry a harlot as a prophetic act demonstrating His own heart towards his beloved, Israel. God said that even though Israel had become like a harlot, He would still marry her and become a Husband to her. It is no coincidence that the heart of the Father for His unfaithful bride is a direct parallel to Yeshua's response to the woman who had been caught in adultery in John chapter eight. The Father and Yeshua are indeed One, in heart and action. So, let us not allow the worldly portrayal of divorce to cast a shadow on God's nature and character. Throughout Israel's unfaithful history, God has never regretted His choice to love Israel. God has no desire for divorce, either spiritually from us, or us from each other.

Back to the issue of the betrothal ritual. In the second phase of the engagement, when the fathers had to decide on the bridal price, the groom's family would set a table with a goblet of wine placed at its center. The fathers of the bride and groom would come together to begin the negotiation over the bridal price. A father might boast that his daughter was a fine girl who could bear twelve sons like the lineage of Jacob. "Look at my daughter. She is not only beautiful, but she can cook and make bread before the sun rises. She knows how to till the fields, tend the flocks, spin wool into cloth, and oy vey, the sons she would give you. How much is such a woman worth? Truly two camels, a tenth of your harvest, ten sheep and twenty goats."

Then the son, the intended groom, would look at his father and say, "Father, if it is possible, let this cup pass before me, but not my will, your will be done." The meaning of this saying was this: should the price for the intended bride be too much, then the groom would "let the cup pass," i.e., not drink from it. But if it was the correct price, then the groom would drink the cup, pay the dowry, and then go to prepare the house for his future bride.

If the price was too much, the groom's father would stop his son and say, "No, son, let this cup pass." Then he would turn to bride's father and say, "Twelve sons you say? But don't you have seven daughters? How could you boast? That is way too much."

The haggling would continue until a price would be agreed upon. During this negotiation, the bride would discover exactly how much she was worth since no one would have wanted to overpay for a bride.

On one of my many trips to Israel, I had a tour guide who was a petite Jewish woman from Tunisia. In Israel, all young men must serve three years and young women must serve two years in the Israeli Defense Force (IDF). When this girl was in the military, one of her many responsibilities was to check on various Bedouin tribes that were still nomadic in the desert. A former teacher of mine with a doctorate in Bedouin studies told me once that if one wished to learn about the culture of ancient biblical times, one needed to study the Bedouin. Their culture is still the closest to those of ancient times. So, as a young Israeli Army officer, while checking on the Bedouin tribes, sometimes my tour guide would be required to enter the men's tent with her senior officer. However, she was never allowed to speak, just be present.

During one of those visits, her commanding officer was having a discussion with the chieftain, so he asked him how much he would pay for his junior officer as a bride. The old Bedouin man politely declined to offer a price. The commanding officer persisted, "A camel?" The chieftain just shook his head. "A few sheep then?" Again, the Bedouin man declined. Exasperated, the officer completely embarrassed his junior officer by asking, "How much then would you give to marry her?" The Bedouin man looked the woman up and down, then pronounced, "Maybe one small goat." The officer asked, "Why just one small goat?" The Bedouin Chieftain responded, "Look at those hips, so small, not good for many children." And there you have it. The tour guide had learned what her bridal value to the Bedouin people was: one small goat.

Looking at Yeshua's prayer in the Garden of Gethsemane through this important cultural understanding greatly changes how we view His last night. Yeshua was not asking His Father if He could get out of being the sacrifice. Yeshua was asking if being whipped, crowned with thorns, humiliated, tortured, and crucified was the correct price for His bride.

Yeshua could not and did not have ulterior motives in paying the bridal price. He chose to pay the price for His bride, whether that bride would ever choose to accept the price or not. Yeshua's choice to accept the Father's terms were not conditional upon a bride who had already made herself ready. When fathers discussed the bridal price, it was in reference to who the woman was in that moment. So, Yeshua chose for Himself the prostitute bride, the ignorant bride, the unclean bride, the imperfect bride, the faithful bride, the sinning bride, the seeking bride, the righteous bride, the reluctant bride, the unfaithful bride, the bride of Israel as well as the bride of the nations.

It is of paramount importance to realize that the betrothal was not just for ancient Israel but for every man, woman, and child of every nation. When Yeshua drank the cup and paid the price upon the cross, it was for all of us. And just like all newly betrothed men in Israel, Yeshua as the bridegroom would go to prepare the place for His bride.

> "In My Father's house are many mansions; if it were not so, I would have told you. I go to prepare a place for you. And if I go and prepare a place for you, I will come again and receive you to Myself, that where I am, there you may be also." (John 14:2–3)

Overwhelming Truth

Is the imperfect bride worth the death of Yeshua? The answer Yeshua received from God wasn't further negotiations or conditional consent, but the Father looked at His Son and said, "Yes, she is worth this price; Son drink this cup." Yeshua, filled with joy, remained in the Garden of Gethsemane and chose to drink the cup. The overwhelming truth of the value of Yeshua's bride was so great, and even though her cost was so high, Yeshua did not run away. But in preparation to freely pay the price, God sent His angels to minister to his Son.

It comforts me to know that even though Yeshua chose to go to the cross freely and to joyfully lay down His own life, He still needed the comfort of heaven to boldly fulfill His obedience in paying the worthy bridal price. Therefore, we should never diminish the huge payment and the enormous physical burden Yeshua endured. Nor should we diminish the compassion of the Father to help His Son in paying such a worthy price for such a valuable bride. In all things, we should feel reverently honored that Yeshua had no hesitation in paying this immense price for us.

> Looking unto Jesus, the author and finisher of
> our faith, who for the joy that was set before Him
> endured the cross, despising the shame, and has
> sat down at the right hand of the throne of God.
> (Hebrews 12:2)

It is not a light thing for a person to discover their true worth. Before Yeshua's sacrifice and before He made you holy and righteous, your value was His life. Many of us may still have doubts, guilt, or shame to feel acceptable of such a cost. However, the Bible is filled with other stories that will give us the confidence of understanding what was, is, and always will be in God's unchanging heart.

Yeshua has fulfilled or will fulfill all of Scripture. As the Messiah, He did what every other prophet did, yet to a greater degree. Abraham is called a man of faith. He is also called the Father of all nations because God promised Abraham that anyone who called our God "Abba Father" would be known as one of his descendants. Yet Abraham was of a very old age, and he and his wife Sarah still didn't have a son of their own. Finally, when Abraham was 100 years old, Isaac was born to them. After some time, God asked Abraham to offer his one true son and heir as a sacrifice to the Lord.

The Scripture says that Isaac was a lad as he walked with his father to go and worship the Lord. Here is what took place as Isaac and Abraham walked up Mount Mariah:

> So Abraham took the wood of the burnt offering
> and laid it on Isaac his son; and he took the fire in
> his hand, and a knife, and the two of them went
> together. But Isaac spoke to Abraham his father and
> said, "My father!"
> And he said, "Here I am, my son." Then he said,
> "Look, the fire and the wood, but where is the lamb
> for a burnt offering?" (Genesis 22:6–7)

Abraham answered his son with a great prophetic word:

> And Abraham said, "My son, God will provide for
> Himself the lamb for a burnt offering." So, the two of
> them went together. (Genesis 22:8)

In Hebrew, this passage can also be translated as God will provide *Himself* as the lamb for the burnt offering. Look at it this way: Mount Mariah is the hill that's directly north of the city of Jerusalem. It was founded by Melchizedek, conquered by King David, and became the home of the First and Second Temples. Isaac, the son of Abraham, walked up this mountain carrying wood on his back. Yeshua also walked up the same mountain carrying His cross (the wood for the sacrifice) on His back. In the same place where Abraham had declared, "God Himself will provide the sacrifice," Yeshua had become the sacrifice.

Next, Isaac would have helped his father prepare the altar, arranging the wood for the fire and preparing himself to be that burnt offering. According to Jewish tradition, Isaac was nearing thirty years of age at this time. How then, could Abraham, who was well over one hundred years of age, subdue his son from becoming the sacrifice? Isaac would have chosen to climb upon the altar, chose to be bound, and chose to lift his head to the sky to expose his neck for the sacrifice.

I know many of you have seen pictures or famous paintings of this Bible story of Abraham holding his knife extended high overhead. A young naked Isaac is bound and afraid. Then suddenly a naked angel appears and restrains Abraham. But this is not the position a man would take to prepare his offering for the Lord. Instead, the knife would have been extremely sharp, able to slice the neck in one clean motion, causing a near-instant death. An adult Isaac would have been bound with his neck extended. Then Abraham would have placed the blade of the knife on his son's neck before God spoke for him to stop.

Think of the confidence that Isaac demonstrated toward his father! In his obedience, he chose to get up on that altar and release his destiny, his very life, into the hands of his father and his father's God. Even though Abraham did not understand why he was asked to sacrifice his only son, Abraham was willing to give to God whatever He had asked of him because of his faithful relationship with the Lord.

> And Abraham stretched out his hand and took the knife to slay his son. But the Angel of the Lord called to him from heaven and said, "Abraham, Abraham!"
>
> So, he said, "Here I am."
>
> And He said, "Do not lay your hand on the lad, or do anything to him; for now, I know that you fear God, since you have not withheld your son, your only son, from Me."
>
> Then Abraham lifted his eyes and looked, and there behind him was a ram caught in a thicket by its horns. So, Abraham went and took the ram, and offered it up for a burnt offering instead of his son. (Genesis 22:10–13)

God did provide an alternate sacrifice that day as an archetype of what would happen on that same hill in the future. As a direct comparison, we can now see how Isaac, being the son of promise for Abraham, freely chose to become the sacrifice and offering for his father, yet God intervened. Whereas, Yeshua, being God's only Son, also chose to be the offering and sacrifice but became the ultimate fulfillment of Abraham's prophecy.

Psalm 23

The Lord the Shepherd of His People
A Psalm of David.

1 The Lord is my shepherd;
I shall not want.
2 He makes me to lie down in green pastures;
He leads me beside the still waters.
3 He restores my soul;
He leads me in the paths of righteousness
For His name's sake.
4 Yea, though I walk through the valley of
the shadow of death, I will fear no evil;
For You are with me;
Your rod and Your staff, they comfort me.
5 You prepare a table before me in
the presence of my enemies;
You anoint my head with oil;
My cup runs over.
6 Surely goodness and mercy shall follow me
All the days of my life;
And I will dwell in the house of the Lord
Forever.

PART 5
Grace is
Our Identity

Putting It All Together

Putting it all together, we now see that your sin, my sin, our sin, did not kill Yeshua. Instead, it gave Yeshua the chance to show that He is Faithful, that He is Love, that He is who He said He was. God wanted a relationship with us that could never be broken, so Yeshua chose to become the sacrifice of sacrifices to satisfy every requirement in the Torah. And then He, Himself, provided a one-sided relational covenant by choosing to pay the price for His beloved, His bride, His people, both Israel and the nations. Yeshua did so freely, not because of our sin, but because He wants an eternal relationship with us. He did it because it was the worthy price for His bride. He did it because He is peace, He is healing, and He is reconciliation. He is also the door for an intimate face-to-face relationship with the Father.

After Yeshua paid the bridal price, as the bridegroom He went to prepare our dwelling in the Father's house. Now the bride must be patient and faithful. The desired beloved must realize that we can no longer have any other lovers or suitors. No one else can betroth themselves to us. Yeshua's death and resurrection ushered the entire world, both Israel and the nations, saved and unsaved, into an arranged marriage with the King of kings. We had no choice in the matter because it was a one-sided covenant made on our behalf by our true Father who loves us so much. This act of grace can never be purchased, bargained for, or deserved. It can only be obtained by believing that it is true.

An arranged marriage can be a scary thought for many. Most western nations do not understand the concept of or practice arranged marriages. The unknown can be scary. Yet, God in His goodness and mercy showed us how to view our own arranged marriage to Him.

The Passover account in the book of Exodus begins with the story of God showing His mercy to Israel. Even though the Israelites didn't know God or His ways, God, with an outstretched arm, brought Israel out of the Land of Egypt, out of the house of slavery. They were to go and to worship Him, live with Him, and be in a personal relationship with Him. Exodus also released the marriage betrothal to Israel. Its chapters are written in the form of a *ketubah*, where God proposed to marry Israel, to protect her, lead her, provide for her, and always be her Husband and God.

Next, there is another tradition for the Jewish community during the Passover. During the Passover week, some Orthodox Jews read a specific book of the Bible called the Song of Songs. The Song of Songs is a book about the great love, strong desire, and the sensual poetry of two lovers. It tells of the bridegroom's love for his beloved and the desire of the beloved for her bridegroom. This book fills us with hope and expectation that not only will our arranged marriage be okay, but it is also going to be filled with desire and passion.

Let's look at the Shulamite woman, who is a representation of the Bride of the Messiah, toward her Beloved, her arranged Husband:

> Let him kiss me with the kisses of his mouth—
> For your love is better than wine. (Song of Songs 1:2)

> He brought me to the banqueting house,
> And his banner over me was love. (Song of Songs 2:4)

Next look at one of the passages that reveal how the Beloved (who could be compared to Yeshua) speaks about his future bride (could be all believers in Yeshua) and the love of His life:

The Beloved
Behold, you are fair, my love!
Behold, you are fair!
You have dove's eyes behind your veil.
Your hair is like a flock of goats,
Going down from Mount Gilead. (Song of Songs 4:1)

Note the Shulamite longing for her arranged Husband, the Beloved. This is both like Yeshua's desire for us and our response to Him, even in our uncertainty about our appearance or the state we are in. The draw of the Beloved is so great, even to the point of being beaten, that the love of these two cannot be quenched:

I sleep, but my heart is awake;
It is the voice of my beloved!
He knocks, saying,
"Open for me, my sister, my love,
My dove, my perfect one;
For my head is covered with dew,
My locks with the drops of the night."
I have taken off my robe;
How can I put it on again?
I have washed my feet;
How can I defile them?
My beloved put his hand
By the latch of the door,
And my heart yearned for him.
I arose to open for my beloved,
And my hands dripped with myrrh,
My fingers with liquid myrrh,
On the handles of the lock.

I opened for my beloved,
But my beloved had turned away and was gone.
My heart leaped up when he spoke.
I sought him, but I could not find him;
I called him, but he gave me no answer.
The watchmen who went about the city found me.
They struck me, they wounded me;
The keepers of the walls
Took my veil away from me.
I charge you, O daughters of Jerusalem,
If you find my beloved,
That you tell him I am lovesick! (Song of Songs 5:2–8)

More Wisdom from a Welsh Shepherd

Our love story involves God, who draws near to us and wants a relationship with us. He paid the price for us, not just for the bride we would become but also because of who we were. He is the One we look to upon the cross and love. Once we have this revelation, how can we ever again use the cross as a weapon or source of shame? How can we try to pay God back for the price He paid for us?

Do you remember Bob, the shepherd from Wales? After he rescued his fearful sheep from the bushes, Bob then carefully lifted each sheep from the brambles. Then Bob pulled all of the twigs out of their wool and grabbed them by their faces to look them in the eye. The helpless sheep, just rescued from certain death, stared back into the shepherd's face. Bob straightened up and asked me, "Do you know what happens next?" Wanting him to go on, I quickly nodded my head. Bob got a gleam in his eye and with a bright smile he said, "They run away and join the other sheep. To this day not a single sheep has ever stopped to say thank you. They don't have to because they are my sheep."

As I stood in a field with hundreds of sheep all around us, a reverent peace came over me. I realized there was a deeper parable that Bob was teaching me. God was using the simple truth of a natural shepherd. If Bob loved and cared for his sheep and worked tirelessly to keep his sheep safe—rescuing them without reservation, never needing to be thanked by the sheep he had been tending—how much more love, acceptance, and understanding does our Great Shepherd have for us? The truth is that our Shepherd has no need for us to come groveling to Him, trying to pay Him back for our transgressions. After all, God does call us His sheep.

> For He is our God,
> And we are the people of His pasture,
> And the sheep of His hand. (Psalm 95:7)

I will never forget the first time Bob took me to meet his sheep. I was so excited just to know and meet such an amazing man. As we stood in the field, he turned to me and said, "Mathew, do you know what the difference is between a good shepherd and a bad shepherd?"

I didn't know much about Welsh shepherds. "I don't know," I said.

Bob smiled. "A bad shepherd doesn't understand the mind of a sheep so he can never understand what a sheep needs." Then he said, "On the other hand, a good shepherd can get into the mind of a sheep and think like a sheep, so he knows exactly what the sheep needs."

I was dumbfounded by the depth of a shepherd's wisdom.

Standing there in another green pasture I realized that Bob's words accurately and simply explained why Yeshua came as a man. Our God and Shepherd cannot only think like a sheep, but He also knows what His sheep need because He became a sheep in the flesh. It was His humility to become a sheep to know us, to think like us, to feel like us, to be tempted like us, and to even struggle like us. As it states in Hebrews:

> For we do not have a High Priest who cannot
> sympathize with our weaknesses, but was in all points
> tempted as we are, yet without sin. Let us therefore
> come boldly to the throne of grace that we may
> obtain mercy and find grace to help in time of need.
> (Hebrews 4:15–16)

A Different Picture

I am genuinely humbled by the lengths God Himself provided to have an everlasting relationship with us. I always wanted to feel worthy, to be worthy, and to do my best to prove my worthiness. However, just like Bob's sheep, we are the sheep of God. He is the good Shepherd, who also came as a sheep in the form of man so that He could always relate to us, be with us, and live in us. Because He so wanted eternal relationships with us, He paid all debts, forgave all sin, and opened the doorway to heaven.

"Immanuel" is one of the many names of God, which means "God with us." Just take a moment to think about how God is with us, God is in us, and we are in God. Sometimes people like to envision a picture of a man standing on the side of a cliff and there's a huge chasm that separates mankind from

God. The chasm is often labeled "sin." Then a huge cross is drawn to show how Yeshua bridged the gap between mankind and God so that people can now cross over to God.

If Immanuel means "God with us," then why do people draw a picture of God far away from us? If God can't live with us because of sin, then how did He approach Adam and Eve after the fall, or ever walk with Peter, James, and John in Israel? If God does live with us, then there is a much greater picture for us to envision. It is a picture of a God who is there around us, revealing His nature to us, and ordering our steps in the hopes that we would have the revelation of who He is. He is not separated by a chasm, but He is patiently waiting for us to recognize the true nature of Him who is dwelling with us. He is not an angry God, a faraway God, or unapproachable God. Instead, He is a loving Father, Shepherd, and Bridegroom.

I like the picture of a man or woman standing alone, but as soon as their hearts are opened and they find Yeshua, they turn around to discover that God has always been with them, longing to be in a personal relationship with them. This God has already declared that they were valuable all along.

That's our God, the God who looks you in the eye and declares you are worthy. You are worthy. It is such a powerful statement. You can never pay for your worth or earn your worth, nor live up to your worth because your value was set by your Father in heaven. If ever you doubt this, look at yourself in the mirror and declare God's eternal truth: You are worthy just as you are!

Walking in a New Identity

I have been in ministry for some time now and have made many mistakes. When I was a young man in Budapest, Hungary, I had no clue as to what I was doing. I thought I was mature and ready to be a rabbi, but I had made a fundamental mistake. I saw myself as the noun—the shepherd, pastor, rabbi. I never understood the Scripture in the book of Matthew:

> "But you, do not be called, 'Rabbi'; for One is your Teacher, the Christ, and you are all brethren. Do not call anyone on earth your 'father'; for one is your Father, He who is in heaven. And do not be called 'teachers'; for one is your Teacher, the Christ. But he who is greatest among you shall be your servant. And whoever exalts himself will be humbled, and he who humbles himself will be exalted."
> (Matthew 23:8–12)

Our identities can never be placed in a title because in the final days there will only be two groups: sheep and goats. The sheep will inherit eternal life, and the goats will be forever separated from God. Those of us who are trained and educated to be pastors, teachers, and rabbis need to remember that we are just like verbs or adjectives. We do the work, service, and love of a pastor, teacher, or rabbi, but ultimately, we are just sheep.

It was so freeing when God removed me from the pedestal of being a pastor and rabbi and returned me to my rightful place as a son. Now, my only delight is in being a child of God. It wasn't always easy for me to live with a simple identity. I felt unclean, unworthy, and a fraud. Then, after receiving the revelation of grace, my life was never the same. I still sin and I still struggle. I still need to be reminded of the abundant, never-ending, fully complete love of God. But now I know that I am just a sheep, belonging to the Lord and He is good.

There are so many encouraging verses in the Bible about our identities. We are overcomers and more than conquerors. God tells us that He knew us before we were in our mother's womb. Return to the very first words God spoke over us, the very words which gave us identity. Read them again. Let your Creator's words renew your thinking and tell you who you are today:

> Then God said, "Let Us make man in Our image, according to Our likeness; let them have dominion over the fish of the sea, over the birds of the air, and over the cattle, over all the earth and over every creeping thing that creeps on the earth." So, God created man in His own image; in the image of God He created him; male and female He created them. Then God blessed them, and God said to them, "Be fruitful and multiply; fill the earth and subdue it; have dominion over the fish of the sea, over the birds of the air, and over every living thing that moves on the earth." And God said, "See, I have given you every herb that yields seed which is on the face of all the earth, and every tree whose fruit yields seed; to you it shall be for food. Also, to every beast of the earth, to every bird of the air, and to everything that creeps on the earth, in which there is life, I have given every green herb for food"; and it was so. Then God saw everything that He had made, and indeed it was VERY GOOD. So, the evening and the morning

were the sixth day. (Genesis 1:27–31)

Do you hear His heart for you? After God had created the heavens and the earth, divided the land from the seas and placed every star in the heavens, created the fish, the birds, the creeping things and all of the other animals, our Creator formed us. The God of gods made us in His image, breathed His Spirit into us, and gave us authority on this earth. Yeshua, continuing the work of his Father, did the same. He did not just give His glory to the disciples who were present with Him, but to everyone who would believe. He gave us the revelation that in Him we have new life and a new spirit. We are made complete in Him.

> "I do not pray for these alone, but also for those who will believe in Me through their word; that they all may be one, as You, Father, are in Me, and I in You; that they also may be one in Us, that the world may believe that You sent Me. And the glory which You gave Me I have given them, that they may be one just as We are one: I in them, and You in Me; that they may be made perfect in one, and that the world may know that You have sent Me, and have loved them as You have loved Me." (John 17:20–23)

Yeshua prayed for you. We know the Father answers every one of Yeshua's prayers. It was through your faith and belief in Yeshua that you received the revelation that He had also made you perfect. He did the work. It was Yeshua's choice alone that He humbled Himself to become the true servant of all. We no longer have to strive to attain that which He already fulfilled on the cross. Yeshua Himself declared it while hanging on the cross:

So, when Jesus had received the sour wine, He said,
"It is finished!" And bowing His head, He gave up
His spirit. (John 19:30)

It is finished! These three short words are filled with so
much power. Satan could never undo it, no demon could ever
change it, and no man could ever live without it. It is the power
of God for the salvation of all who would simply believe. No
prayer, no baptism, no type of service, and no form of payment is
needed. Before He died, Yeshua had withdrawn with His disciples
to the northern part of Israel and asked them who people said he
was. They shared various theories about Him. Then Yeshua asked
His disciples who they thought He was, and Peter responded:

He said to them, "But who do you say that I am?"
Simon Peter answered and said, "You are the Christ,
the Son of the living God." Jesus answered and said
to him, "Blessed are you, Simon Bar-Jonah, for flesh
and blood has not revealed this to you, but My Father
who is in heaven." (Matthew 16:15–17)

In the same way, to this day, that revelation is all that is
needed to be saved. To receive the revelation from the Father that
Yeshua is the Messiah, the Son of the Living God is all that is
necessary to begin your new life with Him, with all of the rights
and privileges of being a beloved child of God.

Conclusion

After Yeshua had been crucified, Mary Magdalene and

Mary, mother of Yeshua, went to the tomb on the third day. Upon their arrival, they discovered that He had risen. Yeshua was placed in a grave so we wouldn't have to be there permanently, but could be raised from the dead to dwell with Him eternally. He went to the Father so we could boldly enter the throne room of grace. We no longer need to be crucified for our sins because He chose to die in our place. We no longer need to pay the price for our transgressions because He became the Sin, Trespass, and Peace Offering. So, we, too, simply need to believe that He is alive today.

We are the worthy Bride of the Messiah. He bought and paid for us. No longer can we have any other master, lover, or suitor for our affections. In Him all striving has ended and all curses have been nullified. We have become new creations. Therefore, our DNA is no longer that of the first Adam and has now been redeemed and made perfect in the New Adam. Yeshua did all of this for us.

God will never leave you. He will never forsake you. He will never remove His Spirit from you. He will never cast you aside. He will never abandon you. He will correct you, guide you, provide for you, heal you, protect you, deliver you, teach you, and discipline you. For all those people who have been given the right to become sons and daughters of the most High God through faith and faith alone, they will be seen as pure, innocent, holy, righteous, and forgiven. That is who we are in Christ for all time. This is what has already been prepared for us and extended to all through the New Covenant of Yeshua.

> For God so loved the world that He gave His only begotten Son, that whoever believes in Him should not perish but have everlasting life. For God did not send His Son into the world to condemn the world,

but that the world through Him might be saved. (John 3:16–17)

Not Quite Finished

What will be your next step? Now that you realize you are His Bride, friend, image, sheep, and creation, what will you do? When you begin to live out your new identity, how can you be a true sheep of God? Let me share two more stories from Bob:

"My sheep hear My voice, and I know them, and they follow Me." (John 10:27)

There are many amazing ministry schools and churches around the world that can help you discover how to hear the voice of God. The first and most important place to start with is the Bible, the actual recorded and written word of God. Next, there are two different revelations that can be useful to you. It is these two revelations that I got from Bob which I wish to share.

One day, I asked Bob how long it would take for his sheep to know his voice. Bob proclaimed, "Once the sheep realizes everything it needs to survive comes from me, it will recognize my voice instantly." The simple truth of that statement is the answer that so many people are longing for. After you know that you are indeed God's sheep, and once you realize everything you need to survive comes from Him, then you will recognize the true voice of our Great Shepherd.

But some might say, "When I pray and cry out, it seems that God doesn't answer my prayers, or maybe I can't hear His answer." Remember when three of Bob's sheep were caught in the bushes and were bleating to be rescued? As I stood in the field, Bob and I could hear the sheep bleating in the distance. Bob saw the concern on my face and said, "The sheep don't know it yet, but they are going to be okay. I don't want to get my clothes all muddy right now, so I will go up to the house and get my work coveralls on before I go rescue them. But if they were in mortal danger, I want you to know that I would go out there in my underwear to rescue them!"

We may cry out, wanting a breakthrough or an answer and wonder, *Where is the Shepherd?* You don't know it yet, but you're going to be okay. Should you be in eternal danger, God would show up in His underwear to rescue you. Remember that His grace is sufficient. God's character will never change. Be reassured that no matter what comes, you are His forever! Whether He speaks or whether He's silent, He will never forsake you nor forget you.

> Yet in all these things we are more than conquerors
> through Him who loved us. For I am persuaded that
> neither death nor life, nor angels nor principalities
> nor powers, nor things present nor things to come,
> nor height nor depth, nor any other created thing,
> shall be able to separate us from the love of God
> which is in Christ Jesus our Lord. (Romans 8:37–39)

A Benediction

I pray that your storms, problems, and life's difficulties be resolved quickly. Until then, may you realize that you are going to be okay. I pray that the revelation of the depth of God's grace will come to you. I pray that your new identity in God will be revealed. May old thinking patterns, strongholds, and anything else that has kept you from the revelation of God's love pass away. I pray that you will become passionate about His grace and that you will pursue Him with all your heart, soul, mind, and strength. In Yeshua's name I pray, Amen.

In addition, here is the blessing God asked Aaron to proclaim over the children of Israel, which I now proclaim over you also:

> And the Lord spoke to Moses, saying: "Speak to
> Aaron and his sons, saying, This is the way you shall
> bless the children of Israel." Say to them:
> > "The Lord Bless you and keep you;
> > The Lord make His face shine upon you,
> > And be gracious to you;
> > The Lord lift up His countenance upon you,
> > And give you peace."
> "So, they shall put My name on the children of
> Israel, and I will bless them!" (Numbers 6:23–27)

If you would like to contact Rabbi Mathew for any speaking engagements, please email him at mathewtoller@gmail.com.

Also, you may follow his author's page on Facebook:
Tales of the Wandering Rabbi

If you have found this book to be helpful,
please let others know by leaving a review on Amazon.

Made in the USA
San Bernardino, CA
20 March 2018